Affordable Housing: Building Bridges to Better Homes

***Legal Notice:-** This book is for informational purposes only. While every attempt has been made to verify the information provided in this book, neither the author nor the distributor assume any responsibility for errors or omissions. Any slights of people or organizations are unintentional and the Development of this book is bona fide. This book has been distributed with the understanding that we are not engaged in rendering technical, legal, accounting or other professional advice. In no event will the author and/or marketer be liable for any direct, indirect, incidental, consequential or other loss or damage arising out of the use of this document by any person, regardless of whether or not informed of the possibility of damages in advance.*

Table of Contents

Introduction:

Welcome to a journey through one of the most pressing issues we face today – our broken housing system. In a world where home is supposed to be a sanctuary, a place of safety and comfort, countless individuals and families find themselves without a roof over their heads or entrenched in a constant struggle to keep their homes. It's emotional, it's challenging, and above all, it's an issue that affects each and every one of us, whether we realize it or not.

Imagine waking up every day with the weight of uncertainty pressing on your shoulders. The fear of eviction, the constant juggling of bills, and the stress of searching for affordable housing can be overwhelming. Today, millions of people are navigating this harsh reality. This book aims to shed light on the intricate web that is our housing system, exploring the far-reaching consequences of its failures. By understanding the factors that contribute to this crisis, we can begin to formulate actionable solutions and create a society where everyone has access to safe and affordable housing.

Throughout these chapters, we will delve into the roots of the housing crisis, dissect the heartbreaking stories of those affected by homelessness, and analyze the policies that have led us to this critical juncture. We'll hear from community members and activists who are tirelessly working to bring about change, as well as innovators who are crafting new models for affordable housing. Each chapter will build on the last, weaving a narrative that not only illuminates our problems but also offers hope and tangible solutions.

We live in a world of contrasts, where luxury and poverty can exist side by side.

The truth is, our housing system is not just broken; it is in dire need of repair and innovation. The issues of housing affordability and homelessness are interlinked, and understanding their connection is crucial if we are to forge a path towards reform. From the people who are slipping through the cracks to the families who are forced to choose between feeding their children and paying their rent, the human stories behind these statistics are what drive the urgency for change.

Moreover, it's essential to recognize that fixing the housing crisis doesn't solely rest in the hands of policymakers or huge corporations. It will take a collective effort from all of us – communities, governments, and private sectors alike – to come together and advocate for a fairer, more inclusive housing landscape. We can create partnerships that empower individuals, support grassroots initiatives, and harness creative solutions that honor the dignity of all people.

In this book, we will:

1. Explore the historical context of our housing issues, giving us a clearer view of why we're in this situation today.
2. Share personal narratives that highlight the pressing need for accessible housing and the impact it has on everyday lives.
3. Delve into the financial concepts that shape housing markets and expose the barriers that prevent people from securing homes.
4. Examine the policies that have failed us and consider ways to reform our systems in a manner that fosters equity.
5. Showcase innovative community projects and national movements that

are already making headway in improving housing access.

6. Encourage you, the reader, to reflect on your role in this crisis and how you can take action to help your community and advocate for change.

From stories of despair to examples of hope, " *Building Bridges to Better Homes*" provides a comprehensive look at the state of our infrastructure, the human stories behind the statistics, and the possibilities that exist for a brighter future. So, let's get started. Together, we can explore the complexities of housing and uncover the solutions that will help us move forward. Everyone deserves a place to call home, and each of us has a part to play in making that a reality.

Chapter 1:

The Roots of the Crisis

Overview

To understand the complex landscape of today's housing crisis, we must first journey back in time. How did we arrive at this precarious situation where homes are increasingly out of reach for so many? From historical policies to economic changes, the roots of our broken housing system run deep and intertwine with issues of race, class, and urban development. This chapter will explore the historical factors that have shaped our current housing policies, the impacts of housing discrimination, and the evolution of zoning laws that further complicate the situation for many Americans.

Historical Context

In the United States, the story of housing cannot be separated from the larger narrative of social inequality. The real estate market has been influenced by a myriad of historical events that have both helped and hindered the dream of homeownership.

- **The Great Migration and Redlining**: After World War II, many Black Americans migrated to urban areas hoping for better economic opportunities. However, they encountered systemic barriers that limited their access to housing. The practice of redlining, which involved denying mortgages to people in certain neighborhoods based primarily on race, meant that Black families were often trapped in impoverished conditions. With the government backing of discriminatory policies, entire neighborhoods suffered from disinvestment.

- **The GI Bill**: While this legislation provided returning veterans with various benefits, including access to low-interest mortgages, it significantly favored white veterans over Black veterans. This discrepancy widened the racial wealth gap and perpetuated segregation in housing markets.

- **Zoning Laws**: The advent of zoning laws in the 1920s was another nail in the coffin for equity in housing. These policies, aimed at controlling land use and maintaining property values, often enforced racial segregation and led to the isolation of low-income communities. Zoning regulations can decide who gets to live where and can prevent lower-income families from accessing better neighborhoods with better schools and amenities.

The Economic Landscape

Economic factors also play a significant role in shaping our housing system. The landscape of inequality has exacerbated the crisis:

- **Rising Housing Costs**: Over the last few decades, housing prices have escalated considerably, outpacing wage growth. The National Low Income Housing Coalition reports that in no state can a full-time minimum-wage worker afford a modest two-bedroom apartment. This gap signals a dire need for affordable housing solutions.

- **Gentrification**: In many urban areas, we see the process of gentrification displacing long-time residents as wealthier individuals move into neighborhoods, driving up property values and rents. While gentrification can lead to revitalization, it often strips communities of their cultural identities and pushes low-income families further away from city centers where they might work.

- **The Impact of the COVID-19 Pandemic**: The recent pandemic has left many families struggling with job loss and unstable income, leading to a dramatic increase in housing insecurity. As eviction moratoriums lift across the country, a wave of evictions poses an ever-growing threat to the already vulnerable populations.

The Role of Policy and Governance

Despite the clear understanding of these systemic issues, policy responses have often been slow or inadequate. Recognizing the need for change is crucial, but it must be matched by a commitment to reform.

- **Policy Gaps**: Limited funding for low-income housing and lack of political will often stymie meaningful change. Affordable housing initiatives remain underfunded, leading to long waitlists for public housing, which, in turn, leaves families stuck in unsafe or unsuitable conditions.

- **Community Action**: Grassroots organizations are at the forefront of pushing for housing justice. They challenge inequitable policies and fight for the rights of marginalized individuals. This chapter will present a few powerful examples of community-led efforts, showing how collective action has the potential to drive real change.

Conclusion

The roots of our broken housing system are intertwined with history, economics, and policy failures. By examining these factors, we can better understand how to address the current crisis and work towards a more equitable future. Recognizing the historical injustices will inform our strategies as we strive to create a housing landscape that uplifts every individual and family, ensuring that everyone has a place to call home.

Chapter 2:

The Faces of Homelessness

Overview

As we move deeper into understanding our broken housing system, it's crucial that we focus on the human aspect of the crisis. Behind every statistic lies a personal story, often marked by resilience, courage, and tremendous struggle. In this chapter, we will meet some of the individuals and families facing homelessness, shedding light on their experiences and the societal factors that contribute to their situations. By highlighting these stories, we bring humanity to the numbers and reveal the urgency of the crisis.

Understanding Homelessness

The term "homelessness" is often viewed through a narrow lens, but in reality, it encompasses a diverse spectrum of experiences. Homelessness can manifest in many forms, including:

- **Chronic Homelessness**: Often marked by long-term or repeated periods of homelessness, this can stem from a combination of mental health issues, addiction, and lack of affordable housing.

- **Situational Homelessness**: Many individuals and families find themselves homeless due to unexpected life events such as job loss, divorce, or illness. This can often be temporary but can also lead to long-lasting consequences.

- **Hidden Homelessness**: This refers to those who may not be living on the streets but are temporarily staying with friends or family, couch surfing, or living in crowded conditions. They may not be counted in traditional homeless statistics, yet they experience significant instability.

Personal Stories

To illustrate the impact of homelessness, let's dive into the stories of a few individuals whose lives have been changed by the housing crisis.

- **Sarah's Journey**: Sarah, a single mother of two, was living in her car after losing her job during the COVID-19 pandemic. While she worked diligently to find employment, the rising costs of shelter and childcare left her in a precarious situation. Sarah shares her experience of bouncing between friends and shelters while striving to maintain some semblance of normalcy for her children. Her story highlights the interplay between job insecurity and housing instability.

- **Marcus's Struggle**: Marcus, a veteran, found himself homeless after struggling with PTSD and addiction. His journey through the systems designed to help him illustrates the gaps that exist in our social safety net.

After years of living on the streets and facing discrimination, he finally found a supportive community that helped him reclaim his life. Marcus's story emphasizes the importance of understanding the individual struggles that accompany homelessness and the need for comprehensive support services.

- **Maria's Family**: The Lopez family has faced eviction multiple times due to rising rent costs. Maria and her husband both work full-time jobs but still find it hard to afford housing in their city. They illustrate how rising rental prices create a cycle of instability and stress, even for working families. The Looming threat of eviction forced them to move frequently, impacting their children's education and emotional well-being.

The Impact of Homelessness

Homelessness affects more than just those who experience it directly. It ripples throughout communities and society as a whole. Public resources are strained as cities and municipalities face increased demand for social services, healthcare, and emergency resources to house and support those affected.

- **Health Consequences**: Health issues are significantly more prevalent among homeless individuals. The lack of stable housing exacerbates mental health issues, increases the risk of chronic diseases, and makes access to healthcare services more challenging.

- **Educational Barriers**: For children, homelessness severely impacts education. Frequent moves and instability can lead to lower academic performance, increased absenteeism, and social isolation. When children lack stable housing, they are also more vulnerable to bullying and stigma at school.

- **Economic Impact**: Communities with high rates of homelessness also face economic consequences. Lost productivity, higher healthcare costs, and increased strain on social services create a burden that can stifle community growth and potential.

Initiating Change

While the challenges are significant, change is possible. There are numerous community programs and policies aimed at reducing homelessness and providing substantial support. These initiatives can break the cycle of poverty and provide pathways to stable housing.

- **Housing First Model**: This approach prioritizes providing the homeless with permanent housing as the first step in addressing the many issues that accompany homelessness. Housing First programs have shown promise by reducing homelessness and improving people's overall quality of life.

- **Strengthening the Safety Net**: By addressing gaps in social services, we can create a system that better supports individuals in need. This includes access to job training, mental health services, and educational resources for children.

- **Advocacy and Activism**: Community advocacy groups continue to push for policies that prioritize affordable housing, safeguard tenant rights, and expand available resources for homeless individuals. In many cities, movements are gaining momentum as families come together to demand action from local governments.

Conclusion

The human stories woven into the fabric of homelessness remind us of the complexity of the issue. By understanding the diverse experiences that contribute to homelessness, we build empathy and encourage collective action to address the crisis. The narratives of individuals like Sarah, Marcus, and Maria provide vital context as we continue our exploration of our broken housing system and consider the policies and practices that can promote positive change.

Chapter 3:

Understanding Housing Affordability

Overview

Now that we've set the stage by examining the human element of homelessness, it's time to delve deeper into the concept of housing affordability. What does it mean when we say that housing is unaffordable? This chapter will break down the key economic and social factors that contribute to the affordability crisis, explore the mathematics of housing costs versus incomes, and discuss the role of wages, rents, and the elusive American Dream of home ownership.

Defining Housing Affordability

Housing affordability is generally defined as spending no more than 30% of a household's income on housing costs. This includes rent or mortgage payments, as well as utilities and other associated expenses. When families spend more than this threshold, they are considered cost-burdened, meaning they struggle to meet their other essential needs, such as food, healthcare, and education.

- **Cost Burden and Severe Cost Burden**: Households that spend more than 30% of their income on housing are cost-burdened. Those paying over 50% face severe cost burden, often leading to difficult choices like skipping meals or forgoing medical care to cover housing costs.

The Numbers Behind the Crisis

To fully grasp the affordability crisis, we must look at the numbers closely:

- **Income vs. Rent Growth**: Over the past three decades, average wages have stagnated while housing costs have skyrocketed. According to a report from the National Low Income Housing Coalition, while inflation-adjusted median renter income has barely budged, rents across the country have surged. In recent years, the gap has widened significantly, leading to increasing rates of cost-burdened and homeless households.

- **The American Dream**: Homeownership has long been championed as a pillar of the American Dream. However, the reality is increasingly obscured by the rising costs associated with purchasing a home. According to the U.S. Census Bureau, the homeownership rate among millennials remains lower than previous generations. Factors such as student debt, high housing prices, and stagnant wages have hindered this path for many young people.

Contributing Factors to the Affordability Crisis

Several key factors contribute to the current state of housing affordability:

1. **Supply and Demand**: Basic economic principles of supply and demand significantly influence housing costs. As urban areas grow and populations increase, the demand for housing often outstrips supply. When the supply doesn't keep up, prices rise, making homes increasingly out of reach for low- and moderate-income households.

2. **Investment and Speculation**: Housing as an investment leads to inflated prices, especially in desirable neighborhoods. Large investors often purchase properties to convert them

into rental units or flip them for profit, driving up costs for those actually seeking homes to live in.

3. **Zoning and Development Regulations**: As discussed in Chapter 1, zoning laws often limit the availability of affordable housing. Restrictions on building multi-family homes or low-income housing developments can increase the shortage. Communities resistant to change often fight against new developments, thereby exacerbating the affordability crisis.

4. **Economic Disparities**: Systemic economic disparities related to race, class, and geographic location deepen the divide in housing affordability. Marginalized communities are often left behind in the housing market,

facing discrimination and fewer opportunities for upward mobility.

Solutions to the Affordability Crisis

Recognizing the affordability crisis is the first step. The next step is brainstorming solutions:

- **Increasing Housing Supply**: One way to combat rising costs is to increase the supply of affordable housing units. Governments and nonprofits can incentivize developers to create low-income housing through subsidies and tax breaks.

- **Rent Control**: Some cities have implemented rent control measures to stabilize housing costs and ensure residents can afford to stay in their homes. Though rent control remains a contentious issue, communities adopting such measures have reported benefits for tenants.

- **Creating Mixed-Income Neighborhoods**: Developing mixed-income communities can help integrate affordable units with market-rate housing, allowing for socioeconomic diversity and reducing overall housing pressure.

- **Enhancing Support for Vulnerable Populations**: Targeted assistance for low-income families, veterans, and those with disabilities can mitigate some of the pressures they face in the housing market. Programs may include housing vouchers, direct rental assistance, and more robust services to support mental health.

Conclusion

Understanding housing affordability is essential for grasping the root causes of our broken housing system. By exploring the numbers and factors at play, we equip ourselves to advocate for effective solutions and policies that can pave the way for a more equitable housing landscape. Through collective action and innovative approaches, we can steer toward a future where everyone has safe and affordable housing options available.

Chapter 4:

The Role of Policy and Governance

Overview

Policies and governance fundamentally dictate the flow of housing opportunities and can either alleviate or exacerbate housing crises. In this chapter, we will examine the various policies that have shaped housing in our society, identify the gaps and shortcomings of existing systems, and explore ways in which we can reframe governance to be more inclusive and effective.

Exploring the Policy Landscape

To understand the role of policy in shaping our housing landscape, it's essential to recognize the key governmental programs and regulations that have influenced housing across the country.

- **Public Housing Programs**: Initiated in the 1930s, public housing was designed to provide safe and affordable housing for low-income individuals and families. While these programs have helped many, they have often struggled with underfunding, poor maintenance, and bureaucratic red tape.

- **Housing Choice Vouchers (Section 8)**: This program assists low-income families in affording housing in the private market by subsidizing a portion of rent. While beneficial, the program has faced limits due to insufficient funding and uneven distribution across geographic areas, leaving many families on waiting lists.

- **Community Development Block Grants (CDBG)**: These federal grants aim to support community development and affordable housing initiatives. However, they often lack consistent funding, and the allocation process can be mired in political concerns.

- **Zoning Regulations and Building Codes**: Local zoning laws profoundly influence housing availability and affordability. Restrictive zoning can limit new housing development or favor affluent neighborhoods, exacerbating segregation and inequality.

Shortcomings of Existing Policies

Despite the noble intentions behind many housing policies, significant shortcomings exist that exacerbate the crisis:

1. **Underfunding and Political Will**: Many housing programs are chronically underfunded, resulting in long waiting lists and inadequate access for those in need. Without political support to prioritize affordable housing, meaningful changes are slow and difficult to achieve.

2. **Bureaucratic Barriers**: The complex maze of regulations can make it challenging for both individuals seeking housing assistance and developers trying to build new

affordable units. Simplifying these processes can facilitate better access to housing options.

3. **Exclusionary Practices**: Policies often inherently favor those with more resources, keeping low-income families in a cycle of poverty. Discriminatory practices within housing policies can further marginalize already vulnerable groups.

Innovative Policy Ideas

Shifting our approach to policy and governance could create a more equitable housing landscape. Here are a few innovative ideas that could help:

- **Inclusionary Zoning**: Mandating that a certain percentage of new housing developments are affordable for lower-income households creates a mixed-income community and broadens access.

- **Rent Stabilization Policies**: Introducing statewide rent stabilization laws can help protect tenants from skyrocketing rental prices, giving them better security in their housing situation.

- **Comprehensive Community Programs**: Housing policy should integrate housing, education, and employment initiatives to create holistic solutions that address interconnected issues.

- **Equitable Tax Incentives**: Restructuring tax incentives to favor affordable housing development over luxury apartments can direct resources to where they are most needed.

Community Engagement and Advocacy

Active community engagement is vital to guiding and shaping housing policy. Grassroots organizations can lead the charge in advocating for fair and just policies that prioritize the needs of those struggling to secure stable housing.

- **Community Organizing**: Grassroots movements bring together individuals who share similar housing concerns and mobilize them for action. This can include protests, petitions, and lobbying efforts.

- **Partnerships with Local Governments**: Collaborating with municipal leaders can facilitate policy changes at the local level that are more responsive to the needs of the community and foster inclusive dialogue.

- **Awareness Campaigns**: Raising awareness about housing issues and mobilizing public support can pressure lawmakers to prioritize affordable housing initiatives and make necessary reforms.

Conclusion

Policies and governance hold immense power in shaping our housing landscape. By examining the existing frameworks, recognizing their shortcomings, and pursuing innovative solutions, we can work towards a housing system that serves everyone equitably. Through advocacy, community engagement, and a push for reform, we can help bring about the positive changes needed in our broken housing system.

Chapter 5:

Community Voices: Stories from the Ground

Overview

As we explore potential solutions and policies, it's crucial to ground our understanding in genuine community experiences. The voices of those currently experiencing housing insecurity offer valuable insights into the challenges they face and the solutions that resonate most. In this chapter, we will share firsthand accounts from community members who have bravely navigated the housing crisis, highlighting their resilience, hopes, and demands for change.

Meeting the Community

To truly understand the impact of our broken housing system, we're taking a closer look at the experiences of those living on the frontlines. Below are a few powerful stories from individuals and families whose voices bring clarity to this complex issue.

- **James' Resilience**: James is a father of three who once had a stable job as a warehouse manager. After he was laid off during the pandemic, he found himself struggling to make ends meet. With limited savings and no job, he faced eviction. James shares how he connected with local organizations that assisted him in applying for financial aid and finding temporary shelter. His journey illustrates the need for supportive services that can step in during crises.

- **Anita's Fight for Stability**: A retired teacher, Anita after losing her husband, suddenly found herself living on a fixed income. Although she had always been able to afford her home, rising taxes and maintenance costs pushed her to the brink of losing her house. She became an active member of a local advocacy group pushing for age-friendly housing policies, showing how community organizing can be a powerful tool for change.

- **The Martinez Family's Journey**: The Martinez family, who fled their home country due to violence and instability, arrived in search of safety. However, they faced numerous challenges in finding affordable housing. With limited English proficiency, they found it difficult to navigate the complex renting process. They became part of a community mentorship program, which helped them understand their rights as tenants and gain access to housing resources.

Impacts of Community Involvement

Community involvement plays a transformative role in shaping housing policies and services. Organizations dedicated to advocating for housing rights can facilitate conversations that drive change.

- **Grassroots Mobilization**: Local groups have mobilized communities, creating campaigns and connecting people to essential resources. Through outreach, they have helped individuals and families find housing assistance and legal protections, illustrating the power of collective action.

- **Providing Education and Resources**: Community organizations often offer workshops and resources to empower individuals with knowledge about tenant rights, budgeting for housing, and accessing social services.

By providing these essential tools, they equip members of the community to advocate for themselves and others.

- **Building Hope and Resilience**: The sharing of personal stories can foster a sense of solidarity and community among individuals facing similar struggles. It can inspire others to speak out and seek assistance, creating spaces where people can find hope and resilience.

The Call for Policy Change

The voices of community members consistently echo a desire for systemic change. Housing justice demands not only immediate assistance but also long-term solutions that address the root causes of housing insecurity.

- **Affordable Housing Development**: Community members call for local governments to prioritize affordable housing projects that are accessible and truly meet the needs of low-income families.

- **Tenant Protections**: The demand for stronger tenant protections, including anti-discrimination laws and eviction protections, resonates throughout the community. Individuals highlight how these policies could create greater stability in their living situations.

- **Investment in Support Services**: Many call for enhanced investment in mental health resources, job training programs, and comprehensive social services that can help individuals address the complexities surrounding housing insecurity.

Conclusion

The stories shared by community members provide critical insights into the realities of navigating our broken housing system. Their voices resonate with resilience and courage, and they highlight the essential role of community involvement in driving change. By listening to these stories and centering the experiences of those most affected, we can better understand the path towards creating a fairer housing landscape.

Chapter 6:

Innovative Solutions: What Works?

Overview

With a clearer understanding of the challenges presented by our broken housing system, it's time to turn our attention towards the innovative solutions being implemented across the country. This chapter will explore a range of successful programs, initiatives, and strategies that are taking root and demonstrating potential for greater housing stability and affordability.

Housing First Initiatives

One of the most effective approaches to addressing homelessness is the Housing First model. This strategy operates on the premise that providing individuals with stable housing is the critical first step in addressing other challenges, such as mental health issues or addiction.

- **Case Studies**: Cities such as Salt Lake City and Houston have implemented Housing First initiatives with notable success. By prioritizing permanent housing for the homeless, these cities have seen significant declines in homelessness rates while reducing the overall costs associated with emergency services and healthcare for homeless individuals.

- **Benefits**: Research indicates that individuals in Housing First programs experience improved mental health, greater stability, and higher rates of employment. This model can reduce the reliance on shelters and emergency services, showcasing a sustainable alternative to traditional approaches to homelessness.

Community Land Trusts (CLTs)

Community land trusts present another innovative solution focused on preserving affordable housing:

- **What Are CLTs?**: A CLT is a nonprofit organization that acquires and holds land for the benefit of the community, ensuring long-term affordable housing opportunities. The trust separates the ownership of land from the ownership of housing, so that when homes are sold, they remain affordable for future occupants.

- **Success Stories**: Cities like Burlington, Vermont, and Atlanta, Georgia, feature successful CLTs that have created affordable housing for low- and moderate-income families. By engaging community members in the development process, these trusts strengthen community ties and promote stability.

- **Benefits**: CLTs help stabilize neighborhoods, prevent displacement, and promote community engagement. Because they prioritize local needs, they can tailor their approaches to fit the unique dynamics of the neighborhoods they serve.

Innovative Funding Models

Funding is often a significant barrier to implementing affordable housing solutions. However, some innovative funding models are emerging to address this challenge.

- **Social Impact Bonds**: These are outcomes-based investments where private investors provide upfront capital for housing and social services. If agreed-upon outcomes are achieved —such as reductions in homelessness or healthcare costs—the government pays back the investors with interest. This model incentivizes investment in preventative measures while reducing taxpayer burdens.

- **Crowdfunding for Housing**: Several startups and nonprofits are tapping into the power of crowdfunding to raise funds for affordable housing projects. This approach democratizes the funding process, allowing community members to invest directly in their neighborhoods, fostering a sense of ownership and commitment.

Zoning and Policy Innovations

Progressive zoning changes and policy reforms are critical to creating environments conducive to affordable housing development.

- **Upzoning**: Some cities have initiated upzoning efforts, which allow for higher density housing in areas traditionally limited to single-family homes. By increasing the number of units in desirable neighborhoods, cities can expand housing options and reduce overall costs.

- **Adaptive Reuse**: This involves repurposing existing buildings—such as old factories or schools—into affordable housing units. This practice not only reduces development costs but also retains the character of neighborhoods. Cities like San Francisco have taken pathways toward effective adaptive reuse policies.

Lessons from Successful Programs

As we examine these innovative solutions, several key lessons emerge that can guide future efforts:

1. **Community Involvement Matters**: Engaging local communities in the conversation about their housing needs is crucial. Solutions are most effective when they reflect the desires and needs of those who are directly impacted.

2. **Collaboration is Key**: Successful housing initiatives often involve partnerships between governments,

nonprofits, and private sectors. Collaborative efforts can leverage resources and expertise, creating a comprehensive approach to tackling housing issues.

3. **Evaluating Outcomes**: Ongoing evaluation of housing initiatives allows for adaptability and change. Programs should collect data and feedback to inform future strategies and improvements.

Conclusion

Innovative solutions are vital to addressing our broken housing system. By examining successful strategies from around the country, we gain inspiration and evidence of what works. These initiatives remind us that greater housing stability and equity are within our reach when communities, governments, and organizations collaborate for change.

Chapter 7:

Building Partnerships: Collaboration for Change

Overview

The complexity of our housing crisis demands collaborative solutions. No single organization or entity can effectively tackle the multifaceted nature of housing insecurity. In this chapter, we will explore the essential role of partnerships in creating meaningful change. By uniting various stakeholders—governments, nonprofits, businesses, and community members—we can create comprehensive strategies that build a more inclusive housing system.

The Value of Partnerships

Creating a stable housing landscape requires collective effort. When various entities join forces, they can pool resources, expertise, and influence, leading to more effective solutions.

- **Government and Nonprofit Collaboration**: Governments can partner with nonprofits to leverage funding and practical resources. For instance, local governments can provide land or funding to nonprofits focused on developing affordable housing, ensuring that resources are directed to where they are needed most.

- **Private Sector Involvement**: Real estate developers and companies can play a vital role in building affordable housing. By participating in public-private partnerships, they can help create housing that meets community needs while benefitting from incentives offered by local governments.

- **Community Engagement**: Engaging community members in partnership efforts ensures that programs reflect the needs and desires of those directly impacted by housing policies. When residents have a voice, they become advocates for their own communities.

Successful Partnerships in Action

To illustrate the potential of collaborative efforts, let's examine a few successful examples of partnerships driving meaningful change:

- **The Home Builders Association**: In many cities, this organization has teamed up with local governments and nonprofits to create homes for low-income families. By streamlining the permitting process and offering incentives to developers, they facilitate the development of affordable units while addressing housing shortages.

- **Banking for the Community**: Financial institutions are increasingly recognizing the social responsibility associated with housing. Several banks have partnered with nonprofits to provide low-interest loans and funding for housing projects geared toward low-income families, demonstrating the financial sector's commitment to solving housing issues.

- **Coalitions for Housing Justice**: Across the U.S., coalitions of grassroots organizations, legal advocates, and service providers work together to lobby for tenant protections, affordable housing policies, and structural changes at every level of government. By combining forces, these coalitions amplify their voices, making it difficult for policymakers to ignore their demands.

Navigating Challenges Together

While partnerships hold great promise for creating effective housing solutions, they also face challenges:

- **Mismatched Goals**: In any partnership, it's crucial to ensure all parties share common objectives. Conflict can arise when stakeholders prioritize disparate outcomes. It's important to facilitate clear communication and alignment of interests from the outset.

- **Resource Allocation**: Ensuring that all partners contribute resourcefully can be a challenge. Some organizations may have more capacity than others, leading to uneven dynamics. Collaborative agreements should outline specific expectations, contributions, and responsibilities.

- **Sustaining Relationships**: Building and maintaining successful partnerships requires ongoing effort. Regular communication, evaluation, and adaptation are needed to ensure partnerships remain effective and aligned with changing community needs.

Conclusion

Partnerships are a critical component of creating effective housing solutions. By uniting diverse stakeholders, we can foster collaboration that drives meaningful change and builds a more inclusive housing system. The collective power of governments, nonprofits, businesses, and community members working together can pave the way toward a future where everyone has access to safe and affordable housing.

Chapter 8:

A Vision for the Future: Dreaming of Home

Overview

As we come to the final chapter of our journey through the broken housing system, it's essential to look toward the future with hope and determination. This chapter will encapsulate the ideas and solutions discussed throughout the book and present a vision of what a reimagined housing landscape could look like. By envisioning a world where everyone has a place to call home, we can inspire action and work toward making that dream a reality.

Dreaming of Home

Home is not simply a physical structure; it represents safety, stability, and belonging. In our vision for the future, we prioritize creating inclusive communities where everyone has access to affordable and quality housing.

1. **Affordable Housing for All**: We envision policies that ensure everyone, regardless of income, has access to safe, affordable housing. This means reformed housing policies that prioritize the development of diverse housing types—multifamily homes, co-housing, and community land trusts—

making it possible for low-income families to thrive.

2. **Comprehensive Support Services**: Our future includes robust networks of support services that address the complexities surrounding housing. This means access to mental health resources, job training, financial education, and comprehensive legal support. By tackling the root causes of housing insecurity, we can prevent crises before they escalate.

3. **Community Empowerment**: We envision empowered communities where residents are actively involved in decision-making about their housing and neighborhoods. This means trust-building initiatives that allow community members to voice their concerns and desires, shaping developments that reflect their needs.

4. **Sustainable Development**: Our vision includes an emphasis on sustainable housing practices that respect our planet. Innovative designs, energy-efficient features, and environmentally friendly materials will ensure that our homes are not only affordable but also sustainable for future generations.

Turning Vision into Reality

While our vision extends toward the future, making it a reality will require actionable steps and ongoing efforts:

- **Policy Advocacy**: To enact lasting change, we must advocate for progressive policies at local, state, and federal levels. This means supporting candidates and initiatives that align with our vision of accessible housing for all.

- **Grassroots Movements**: Building a large-scale movement requires mobilizing individuals across various community sectors. Grassroots efforts can effectively raise awareness, impact local decisions, and galvanize support for affordable housing initiatives.

- **Collaboration Across Sectors**: As outlined in previous chapters, collaborative efforts involving diverse stakeholders—governments, nonprofits, businesses, and community members—are fundamental to bringing our vision into focus. This collaborative mindset must be integrated into all housing initiatives, ensuring comprehensive solutions for diverse challenges.

A Hopeful Closing

The journey through our broken housing system has illuminated the challenges, resilience, and the possibilities that exist within our communities. By envisioning a future that prioritizes accessible, affordable housing for all, we inspire hope and action.

This is not merely a dream, but a goal we can work toward collectively. Every individual plays a role in driving toward a more equitable future. Our broken housing system can become a healed and thriving one with collaborative efforts, innovative solutions, and sustained advocacy. Let's embrace this vision together, for every person deserves a place to truly call home.